Consulting Report

Strategy Recommendations for Dabur

Madhavi C Vasanta[1] & Halime Temel Nalın[2]

1 SVP-CONSULTING, Pagwon, Hyderabad, India.

2 Assistant Professor, Bulent Ecevit University, Department Of Business, Zonguldak,Turkey.

About:

The consulting report gives to-the-point customized recommendations for Dabur's future business strategies. We hope that Dabur finds a new way to make good inroads into future globalized tightly competitive business.

1. Financial Strategies

1.1 Cost-cutting measures

The increasing complexity of financial markets has created by financial innovations and financial risks. Financial decisions have substantial effects on business competitiveness. But it is necessary to adapt financial strategies to company characteristics. Financial management consists of three interrelated kinds of decisions: investment policy, financing policy and dividend policy.

Investment decisions are those which determine how scare funds available committed to the projects and which can range from acquisition of a plant to the acquisition of another entity. Financing decisions are relate to acquiring the optimum finance to meet financial and working capital effectively management. Working-capital includes management of short-term assets and liabilities in a way that ensures the adequacy of resources for company operations. Dividend decisions are related to the determination of how much and how frequently cash can be paid out from the profits of an entity as income or income for its proprietors (Ogilvie, 2009). The financial concepts most relevant to strategic planning are those dealing with firms' capital investment decisions, and finance theory (Myers, 1984). All companies financial environment is a main factor for their success, especially small companies forced by financial limitation to be highly efficient in allocating their scarce resources in order to maximize profits and make sustainability.

Financial strategy as the area of managerial policy that determines the investment, finance and dividend distribution decisions, which are accepted as preconditions of shareholder wealth maximisation. Each type of decision can also be subdivided into two broad categories; longer term (strategic or tactical) and short-term (operational) (Hill, 2009).

Financial strategies aim to improve their market value and lower their cost of capital. It also represents a path to achieve and maintain business competitiveness and makes a company being a world class organization. Financial strategies are goals, patterns or alternatives designed to improve and optimize financial management in order to achieve corporate results. (Salazar et al, 2011). Appropriate financial strategy can be designed to complement the corporate strategy and add value to a company.

Financial strategy has two components (Bender and Ward, 2009):

- Raising the funds needed by an organization in the most appropriate manner.
- Managing the employment of those funds within the organization.

Financial strategy helps to improve the efficiency and competitive power of companies. There are some potential benefits global companies about financial matters:

- Improving quality of accounting report
- Reduced investment in working capital
- Faster close of financial transactions
- Clear identification of cost saving
- Reduced cost of capital
- Improving the organization performance
- Improving capital efficiency

- Coordination between the finance strategy and the business strategy
- Potential to meet key stakeholder requirement
- Recognising threats and risks.

    Financial strategy over the life cycle is shown in Table 1.

Table 1: Financial Strategy over the lifecycle

Growth	Launch
Business risk high	Business risk very high
Financial risk low	Financial risk very low
Funding equity	Funding equity
Dividend payout nominal	Dividend payout nil
Growth high	Growth very high
P/E high	P/E very high
Eps low	Eps nominal
Share price growing and volatile	Share price growing and volatile

Maturity	Decline
Business risk medium	Business risk low
Financial risk medium	Financial risk high
Funding debt	Funding debt
Dividend payout high	Dividend payout total
Growth medium/low	Growth negative
P/E medium	P/E low
Eps high	Eps declining
Share price stable with limited volatility	Share price declining and volatile

Reference: Bender and Ward, (2009) Corporate Financial Strategy, 3rd Edition. Elsevier, London England.

The supply chain management Dabur is a key factor impacting sales, profitability and net working capital. An efficient supply chain system helps in value creation for the cost reduction in two important ways. These are: (i) Positive impact on sales created by improved service reducing investment in inventories and increasing accounts payables. (ii) Cost management: Lower inventory levels result in lower carrying cost. Another significant tool of cost reduction used by Dabur is "value engineering" to identify and develop more cost effective materials. Research and development activities have also helped in reducing the time of processing which has increased productivity (Ahuja and Gupta, 2007).

The economic slowdown is leading to Dabur Company to explore new product areas with an eye toward reaching more customers. FMCG companies to spend more on advertising. Dabur Company major is likely to experience a margin squeeze and weak growth in sales volumes. It is crucial that the Dabur should focus on global buying, operating margins and capital efficiency, aggressive roll out of new variants, extensions and brand restaging. Dabur has to diversify suppliers to improve their negotiating position and minimize supply risks.

Significant online discounts will continue to attract consumers, as will the ease of shopping, easier return policies and convenient navigation on websites and loyalty programs. Innovations such as cost optimization through warehouse and logistics management are expected to revolutionize the e-commerce market and enable companies to improve profit margins. Dabur should increase sales on their website.

Dabur Company also should focus on the management of raw material inflation, the reduction of waste, effective capital expenditure, operational performance measurement, product and customer profitability management, innovation and global supply chain management.

1.2 Investment Opportunities

Investment opportunities play an important role in the theory finance. The mix of a company's assets and its investment opportunities affects its capital structure, the maturity and covenant structure of its debt contracts, its dividend policies, its compensation contracts and its accounting policies (Adam and Goyal, 2000). The capital budgeting process defines the set and size of a firm's real assets, which in turn generate the cash flows that ultimately determine its profitability, value, and viability (Gervais, 2009). Finance theory stresses cash flow and the expected return on assets. The firm's investment opportunities compete with securities that stockholders can buy (Myers, 1984).

Financing decisions can concern value creation process influencing efficient investments decisions according to the existence of conflict of interest between managers and firm's financial stakeholders (shareholders and debt holders) and affecting the relationship with non-financial stakeholders, as suppliers, competitors, customers, etc. (La Rocca et al, 2008).

Investing in different market is about taking and managing risks and problems. These problems are as follows (Randøy et al, 2001: 660-661):

- Asymmetric information available to investors resident in different countries. This includes not only financial data on corporations but also the analytic methods used to evaluate the validity of a security's price.
- Different tax regulations, especially with regard to the treatment of capital gains and double taxation of dividends.
- Regulation of securities markets.
- Alternative sets of optimal portfolios from the perspective of investors resident in one equity market compared to investors resident in other equity markets.
- Different agency costs for firms located in bank dominated markets compared to firms located in the Anglo-American markets.
- Different levels of financial risk tolerance, such as debt ratios, in different countries.

- Differences in perceived foreign exchange risk, especially with respect to operating and transaction exposures.
- Takeover defences that differ widely between the Anglo-American markets, characterized by one share-one vote norms, and other markets featuring dual classes of stock and other takeover barriers.
- The level of transaction costs involved in purchasing, selling, and trading securities.
- Political risk such as unpredictable government interference in capital markets and arbitrary changes in rule.

For Dabur

Fast-Moving Consumer Goods (FMCG) sector is a very high competitive sector with more players coming in the fields of personal care, oral care and skin care. Consumers are very price sensitive in this industry. The FMCG sector changes fast and is constantly evolving. FMCG are products that are sold quickly and at relatively low cost. The market size of FMCG in India is expected to grow from US$ 30 billion in 2011 to US$ 74 billion in 2018. In January 2014, consumer inflation reached 8.79 percent, while the economy grew by just 4.5 percent over the previous year. Economic slowdown in India, together with high inflation, is expected to further drag down consumer demand.

Dabur Corporation is one of India's leading FMCG Companies and a well-developed multinational consumer goods company with interests in hair care, oral care, health care, skin care, home care and foods that conducts business in Nepal, Bangladesh, the Middle East, North & West Africa, European and the US countries. Dabur's products have a huge presence in the overseas markets and are today available in over

60 countries across the globe. Dabur's overseas revenue accounts for over 30% of the total turnover. Dabur also has strong manufacturing capability with 14 manufacturing units spread in India and abroad. In financial year 2013, despite an increasingly challenging economic environment, the company continued to deliver strong results. Its annual revenue is INR 61460 million and Dabur has witnessed exponential increase in market capitalization over the years and has crossed the US$ 5 billion mark in terms of market capitalization. Dabur has been able to drive strong growth in spite of a challenging environment Table 2 presents Dabur's financial indicators during 2009-2013.

Table 2: Key financial indicators of the Dabur Company

Years	2009	2010	2011	2012	2013
EBITDA (INR mil)	5,170	6,670	8,330	9,480	11,240
EBITDA (%)	18.4%	19.7%	20.4%	17.9%	18.3%
Net Sales (INR mil)	28,050	33,910	40,770	52,830	61,460
Profit after Tax	3,910	5,010	5,690	6,450	7,630
PAT Margins (%)	13.9%	14.8%	14.0%	12.2%	12.4%
Market Capitalization (INR mil)	85,380	1,37,820	1,67,220	1,85,360	2,38,870
Earnings per share (EPS)	4.5	5.8	3.3	3.7	4.4
Return on Net Assets Ratio %	53.64	47.46	53.29	40.78	37.44
Net fixed asset	5,590	6,770	15,510	16,680	16,740

Net fixed asset turnover	5.2	5.2	5.5	6.0	5.8
Dividend per share	1.8	2.0	1.2	1.3	1.5
Dividend Payout Ratio %	38.83	38.74	34.73	35.19	35.16
Book Value per Share	9.5	10.8	8.0	9.9	12.2
Current Liabilities & Provisions	8,050	9,200	14,580	13,840	14,120
Debt/Equity Ratio(D/E)	0.16	0.28	0.19	0.75	0.80

EBIDTA is a measurement of a company's operating profitability and cash flow statement. Both EBITDA and profit after tax shows improvement in fiscal 2013 over the previous financial years, despite inflationary headwinds. There has been a significant improvement in operating margin (EBIDTA/Total sales), which grew from 17.9 per cent in 2012 to 18.3 per cent against industry average being around

11-12 per cent in 2013. Profit After Tax (PAT) increased to INR 7634 mil in fiscal 2013 as against INR 6449 mil in fiscal 2012, up by 18.4%. Net profit margin (PAT/Total sales) also grown from 12.2% percent in 2012 to 12.4% per cent in 2013. However this raise is not adequate for the Dabur Company. Improved margins have been primarily driven by two factors. First, due to efficiency gains at our plants translating into better operating margins be it wastage reduction, fiscal incentives or economies of scale. Second, procurement led initiatives that have resulted in decline in material costs as per cent of sales in spite of an inflationary environment.

Dabur achieved strong growth in sales and profits during fiscal year of 2013 with its sales crossing the INR 61,460 mil. Annual net sales are up by 16.3 percent in 2013. The company's new sales force structure has significantly enhanced channel throughput and productivity.

The net fixed asset turnover ratio measures the company's effectiveness in generating sales from its investments in plant, property, and equipment. The net fixed asset turnover was 3.3 %

decreased in 2013 according to previous year, this may not be a serious problem if the Dabur has just made an investment in fixed asset to modernize. Dabur has managed to pay high dividends and has been able to grow their earnings consistently as well. The book value of shares of Dabur showed a substantial improvement during the period 2009-2013. The financial leverage of Dabur increased during the period 2009- 2013.

During fiscal 2013, the net working capital of Dabur improved to 18 days of sales as compared to 25 days in 2012. There were improvements in inventory and receivables management, which were reflected in reduction at both inventory days and days sales outstanding (DSO). In terms of return ratios, ROIC (Return on Invested Capital) increased to 38.1% in fiscal 2013 as compared to 34.0% in fiscal 2012. Return on Equity (ROE) was at 36% in fiscal 2013.

The Company incurred Capital Expenditure of INR 2348 mil during the fiscal 2013 which was invested in expansion of manufacturing capacities in different countries (India, Bangladesh, Sri Lanka, Egypt and Nepal) for regular maintenance expenditure. Material, advertisement and other costs increased in 2013.

Dabur's International Business continued on the strong growth trajectory growing by 17.1% to INR 18,920 mil in fiscal 2013. Dabur's International sales reached 36% in Middle East, 22% in USA, 21% in Africa, 17% in Asia and 4% in other countries.

2. Market Strategies

Dabur needs to increase its reach and spread in terms of customer segments and geographies, not only global but also domestic. The glocal distribution should be such that the products become 'in-customers'-hands' option rather than top-of-the-mind recall. Every buyer should get the product without asking for it. Buyers don't often recall brands and names for certain common products like salt, toothpowder, toothpaste, combs, mirrors etc. as long as the product serves the purpose of meeting the need. Advertising and campaigns do not make much of a difference to rural and urban folks alike who look for a simple product meeting their daily needs or who don't have time to pay attention to the airing ads. Marketing helps those who need to establish themselves or expand but results can be achieved with better logistics and distribution for existing players. A small shop in a village should be equipped with Lal Tail and Janma Ghunti more than Real Juices for the folks living there. They trust traditional therapies of keeping well more than the modern methods of keeping fit with juices and olive shampoo. Dabur's mission of celebrating life meets the goals of all alike – poor and rich, young and old, and men and women. A group of village folks can live without a bottle of almond oil but cannot live without a bottle of gripe water. A working mother cannot live without a pack of Odonil but can live without lozenges. Target the right product to the right segment at the right time – should be the marketing strategy.

2.1 Product Strategies

Dabur's products cater to wide variety of meeting user needs like healthcare, hygiene, skin care, hair care, beauty, foods, and fragrance for all ages including infants, old people, teenagers, young adults, children, and grown-ups across male and female genders.

Product packaging is important to make high volumes in sales and margins. Some products cannot be sold unless prescribed. Some products can be offered as attractive packages. If a cough syrup is acute for meeting an ethical health need, Babool toothpaste is segmented for meeting general hygiene needs. In a remote village in India, toothpaste can be sold in family saving package at low price or be bundled with hair oil in an economy pack. The buyers can find it a useful combo purchase.

Segmentation-wise product offering is next step to making higher margins. Honey and Real juice are the real needs for a busy working mom in a city but not the real needs for a lower-than-middle-income earner in a village. The availability and distribution of the products are hence not much relevant to a village but to a city. In each country, Dabur should identify the segments of developing towns, cities and metros as against the tranches of rural populace in villages or slums. That saves upon unnecessary marketing costs. Why do you want to spend $10000 in promoting smooth and silky shampoo in a village when the residents are happy with a local reetha powder? Offer but don't thrust or force products upon customers.

2.2 Competitor Strategies

Dabur has multiple competitors in different segments. If the overall umbrella brand competes with the likes of Hindustan Lever, ITC, and Procter & Gamble, the product-wise brand competes with the like of Colgate, CavinKare, L'Oreal, and Coca-Cola. The competition should be such that Dabur is able to collaborate with P&G in getting it to its loyal customers and offer co-branded products. At the same time, Dabur should be able to respond to ITC's moves of expanding in the food segment, with, say, packaged fruit or jam or half-cooked curries as against the fully cooked ones that have shorter shelf-life. Next, Dabur should be able to create first-mover advantage in remote places glocally. Price-wars, branding wars and market share wars are common. Dabur cannot achieve a monopoly but nevertheless it can become one of the top three players in the consumer segment, that keeps switching loyalties and that keeps trying new products.

Compete, collaborate, cooperate and play with the competitors to create win-win scenarios that reduce the risk of operating in a market to a minimum. A product like Chyawanprash, honey and rose-water are known for Dabur, just as photo-copying is known for Xerox. Compete with others on these products by offering economy savings packages of bundled products. Chyawanprash is a health product and Dabur has the best buyer-loyalty. Honey is assessed for its quality and Dabur competes for its purity. Rose-water is again a beauty and health product that is adjudged on its purity and originality. A fake rose-water bottle can be made out by its smell, side-effects on skin or taste. Dabur is again known for its quality here. That does not mean that others cannot achieve the quality. However Dabur has the advantage of first-mover or leader in these product examples. Repeat the success here and replicate it on other product categories.

Dabur should go for mergers & acquisitions to achieve synergies of technovation. Hair oil does not need technology but P&G may have technology to achieve better business intelligence results, and product adaptability needs to changing times. Hair oil should not be sticky and too fragrant for working women but it should nourish the hair at all times. Geeks might prefer stylish trend-oriented hair oil that can substitute the need for a hair gel. Dabur's oil might cater to the semi-urban and rural masses. Collaborating and cooperating with P&G, say, might make exotic coconut-almond non-sticky hair style oil as a competing product against gels.

REFERENCES

Accenture (2014) India in 2014 Creating Value with Speed and Quality: The New Imperative.

Narender L. Ahuja and Sweta Gupta (2007) "Dabur India-Working Capital and Cost Managemen"t, Global Business Review, 8 (2): 335-350

Adam, T. and V. Goyal, 2000, The investment opportunity set and its proxy variables: Theory and evidence, Working paper, Hong Kong University of Science and Technology.

Bender, Ruth and Ward, Keith (2009) Corporate Financial Strategy, 3rd Edition. Elsevier, London England.

Dabur website: www.dabur.com, accessed February 2013.

Hill, Robert Alan (2009) Strategic Financial Management: Exercises, Hill & Ventus Publishing.

La Rocca, M., La Rocca, T. and Gerace D. (2008) "Relation Between Capital Structure and Corporate Strategy", The Australasian Accounting Business & Finance Journal, 2(2).

Gervais, Simon. (2009). Behavioral Finance: Capital Budgeting and Other Investment Decisions. Fuqua Business School Duke University.

Myers, S.C. (1984). "Finance Theory and Financial Strategy" Interfaces, 14 (1) pp. 126-137

Ogilvie, John (2009) CIMA Official Learning System Management Accounting Financial Strategy.

Randøy Trond, Oxelheim, Lars and Stonehill Arthur (2001) "Corporate Financial Strategies for GlobalCompetitiveness", European Management Journal 19 (6): 659–669.

Salazar, Alejandra López; Soto, Ricardo Contreras; Mosqueda, Rafael Espinosa (2011) The impact of financial decisions and strategy on small business competitiveness, Global journal of business research: GJBR. 6 (2): 93-10.

www.ingramcontent.com/pod-product-compliance
Lightning Source LLC
Chambersburg PA
CBHW070734180526
45167CB00004B/1744